AF583603

Resilience

written by
Zanni Louise
art by
Missy Turner

FIVE MILE

Hi, I am Jack.
My name
is Lila!
Hola, I am Mina.

I am Li Wei.
I'm Rosie ...
... and this is Freckles!

A big heart helps you care for the world, care for yourself, and care for others.

But how do you grow your heart?

One ingredient you can use to grow your heart is resilience.

What is resilience?
There are many ways
to be resilient ...

Resilience is bouncing back from difficult moments.

Li Wei loves bushwalking with his family on Sundays. Today, they walk through a forest that burnt black in the bushfire. New leaves sprout from every trunk.

The new leaves remind Li Wei that he bounces back when things don't go his way.

Like when he didn't get picked for the soccer team.

Or when he lost the card game.

Or when he fell and split his chin.

He kept going.

Just like these trees.

Resilience is riding the wave of your feelings.

It's Rosie's birthday.

She imagines her perfect day.
Pony rides at the fair.
Face painting. Cupcakes
for all her friends!

Pitter patter.

Oh no, rain! Rosie's party will be cancelled!

Rosie's heart sinks to the bottom of the sea.

Then Rosie takes a deep breath and makes a new plan.

Snip snip!
Neigh!

Rosie's friends laugh when Rosie the pony trots into the living room!

Resilience is finding strength to stand up for yourself.

Kids run in circles, playing tag.
'Can I play?' asks Mina.

'No!' says a boy.

Mina feels sad. She wants to hide,
but knows it's important to say something.

'I don't like being left out,' Mina tells the boy.

She starts her own game of tag with her good friends.
Later, they play leap frog.

Resilience is knowing how you feel and what to do with that feeling.

Jack's brother Zane is very sick. He needs special medicine and spends a lot of time in hospital.

'I don't want to see Zane today,' says Jack. But really, Jack does want to see him. And mostly, he wants Zane to be better.

‘I’m scared,’ Jack tells Dad.

Dad hugs Jack. ‘So am I,’ says Dad. ‘It makes sense to be scared.’

Zane beams when Jack gives him his drawing. Jack feels stronger now.

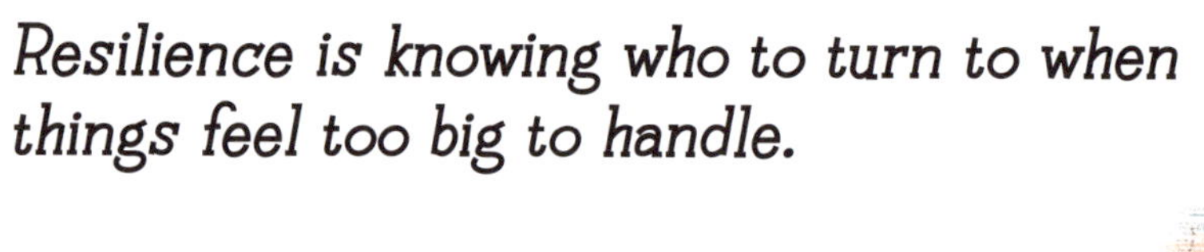

Resilience is knowing who to turn to when things feel too big to handle.

Lila is worried about Mina.
Mina sits alone at recess.
She doesn't eat her lunch.

Lila tells Miss Rachel,
their favourite teacher.
She knows Miss Rachel cares.

‘A good friend notices when their friends need help,’ Miss Rachel tells Lila.

Later, when Lila sees Miss Rachel chatting with Mina, Lila is glad she reached out for her teacher’s help.

You can't always change your situation. But when you are resilient, you stretch like a rubber band.

Mina is moving. Her bedroom is packed in boxes. Mina loves this house. She loves her garden. Her best friend lives next door.

'I'm not going,' Mina tells her mum.

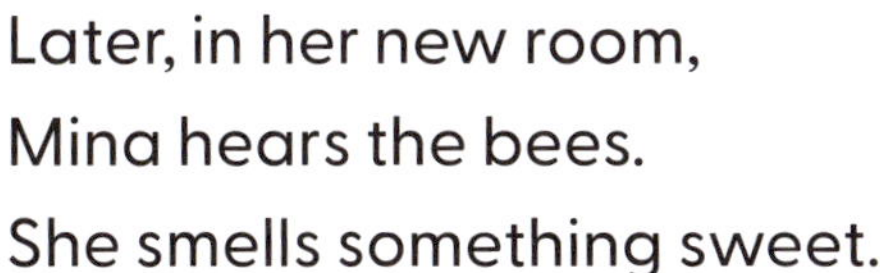

Later, in her new room,
Mina hears the bees.
She smells something sweet.

Mina makes a clover crown for her best friend.

I miss you. Visit soon! writes Mina.

Sometimes you can learn resilience from others.

Li Wei can't sleep. He misses Smoky, his pet rabbit. He creeps out of bed.

He knows Mum misses her family, who live far away. Maybe she can help.

Li Wei listens to Mum tell stories about her hometown. She shows him pictures. 'I hold everything in here,' says Mum, holding her heart.

Li Wei holds his heart. 'I'll hold Smoky in here too,' he says.

Like a flower growing through a crack in the pavement, you are often more resilient than you realise.

Jack dances in his living room.
He dances in his garden.

When Jack enrols in ballet class, he's the only boy. Some kids tease Jack.

His chest aches. He so wants to dance.
So he does.
Jack knows that doing what he loves makes him happy. And that is more important than what some people might think.

Resilience can be something you can grow with time. With patience.

Rosie's parents live in different homes now. Rosie lives with Mum during the week, and Dad on weekends. Her life seems broken.

But Rosie sees her parents are happier now.
And there are things she likes about both homes.

TV nights with Mum.

Ice-cream Sundays with Dad.

Rosie imagines her new life is a tree growing new leaves. New flowers. Her branches reach in new directions.

Resilience comes from inside.
It can come from outside too.

From your friends. Your community. Your teachers. Your parents and carers.

Resilience can be something you learn. And something you grow.

When you are resilient, you cope when things are tough.

You look after your heart.
You change.
You reshape.
Just like a tree.

Resilience helps your heart grow, so you can look after the world, yourself and each other.

Can you think of a time you've been resilient?

Let's talk about resilience

Can you remember a time when you were resilient?

Carpell educator and community worker
'I always wanted to tell my strict dad that I loved him, but was too scared. One day, I pushed aside my fears. I looked at him, and cried, "I love you Dad". Dad cried too. It was such a relief. After that, we could just be ourselves with each other.'

Chrissie child behaviour expert
'When I was 10, I was playing hide-and-seek and somehow managed to get lost in a strange neighbourhood. It was getting dark and I didn't know anyone. I started to cry, but knew I had to be resilient and find a solution. I found a house with bike helmets on the front step – signs a family lived there. I took a big breath and asked for help. The family helped me find my home.'

Melissa principal
'I could not be a successful principal without resilience. Resilience is part of my everyday, I practise it, teach it and model it. I believe each hurdle we jump only gives us opportunity to grow, become stronger and ultimately be more resilient.'

Andy designer
'When something goes wrong and I'm feeling stressed, I sit and take deep breaths until I feel calm. I then turn my focus to solving the problem. Taking those moments to breathe and think has really helped me to overcome tricky situations.'

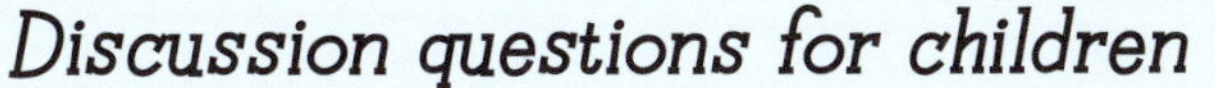

Discussion questions for children

Resilience helps us deal with tricky situations. It helps us grow and learn, even when things get tough. We all have resilience inside us, but we also need help from the people we love.

- Have you faced any tricky situations lately? Maybe there has been a big change in your life or you've had to do something that was really hard.
- How did you feel when you were dealing with that tricky situation? What did you notice in your body? Did you have any worries?
- What did you do that helped you get through the tricky situation?
- Who helped you get through it? What did they do that was helpful?
- Tell me about someone else you know who is resilient. How do they get through difficult situations? If you don't know, maybe you can ask them!

Notes for parents and carers

Resilience is the ability to cope with challenges, adapt to change and bounce back from adversity. Children have an immense capacity for resilience, but they also need us to create an environment in which resilience can grow.

Resilience can change over time, depending on your child's developmental stage and what is happening in their life. Resilience can also look different for every child. Some children may adapt quite easily, whereas others may be more sensitive to stress and need some extra support.

The relationship between a child and their caregivers forms the foundation for resilience. When children have a network of strong, supportive relationships, they are better equipped to deal with stress. Children also need to learn resilience skills, so they have the courage to explore, take risks and cope with future challenges.

Tips for nurturing resilience in children

- Take time to listen to your child and understand their emotional world. Talk to them about their day and any challenges that came up. Sometimes challenges that seem small to us can feel overwhelming for a child. Acknowledge their emotions and allow them to experience whatever feelings arise.
- Teach your child how to recognise and name their emotions, and find ways to manage them. Simple skills, such as taking some slow, deep breaths, can really help children handle big feelings. Teach them how to deal with feelings by modelling positive coping strategies when you feel challenged or overwhelmed.
- Encourage your child to seek support from trusted adults when things get tough. Nurture their social skills to build positive relationships, which will in turn support their resilience.
- Explore age-appropriate stories of resilience with your child. These can be stories from your life or the lives of family members, and stories of people from diverse backgrounds. Encourage your child to ask questions and learn from the people around them. Talk about times when your child has been resilient and what they learnt about themselves.
- Help your child approach problems with a curious and open mind. Give them the space to experiment with different solutions and strategies, so they learn how to be flexible. Teach them to persist with difficult tasks, even when they feel frustrated or they make a mistake. Encourage them to use positive coping statements that focus on their strengths, such as 'I can do this' and 'I will keep trying'. Explain that difficult experiences can be useful because they help us to learn and grow.

Dr Ameika Johnson Child Clinical Psychologist

Also available in this book series

Honesty

Honesty is talking to yourself and others truthfully.

There are many ways to be honest ...

Persistence

Persistence is never giving up, even when things get tough.

There are many ways to be persistent ...

Courage

Courage is stepping towards things we think are scary or difficult.

There are many ways to be courageous ...

Kindness

Kindness is being generous with our words, our actions and our heart.

There are many ways to be kind ...

Made with love by the team at

FIVE MILE

Alex, Niki, Rocco, Graham, Jacqui, Claire, Amy, Lyndal & Emily

Five Mile,
the publishing division
of Regency Media
www.fivemile.com.au

First published 2021

A catalogue record for this book is available from the National Library of Australia

Printed in China 5 4 3 2